ABOUT THE AUTHORS

James Patterson is one of the best-known and biggest-selling writers of all time. His books have sold in excess of 350 million copies worldwide. He is the author of some of the most popular series of the past two decades – the Alex Cross, Women's Murder Club, Detective Michael Bennett and Private novels – and he has written many other number one bestsellers including romance novels and stand-alone thrillers.

James is passionate about encouraging children to read. Inspired by his own son who was a reluctant reader, he also writes a range of books for young readers including the Middle School, I Funny, Treasure Hunters, House of Robots, Confessions, and Maximum Ride series. James has donated millions in grants to independent bookshops and has been the most borrowed author in UK libraries for the past ten years in a row. He lives in Florida with his wife and son.

Maxine Paetro has collaborated with James Patterson on the bestselling Women's Murder Club, Private, and Confessions series. She lives with her husband in New York State.

THE ONE WHO KNOWS THE SECRETS IS THE ONE WHO HOLDS THE POWER. CAN NYPD RED FIND THE TRUTH BEFORE A CITY EXPLODES?

JAMES PATTERSON

THE WORLD'S BESTSELLING THRILLER WRITER

& MARSHALL KARP

NYPD RED 5

A shocking attack

A city on red alert

PLEASE TURN THE PAGE FOR A PREVIEW.

THERE WERE ONLY four words beneath the tattoo of the Grim Reaper on Aubrey Davenport's inner left thigh. But they spoke volumes.

Death is my aphrodisiac

And nowhere in the entire city was her libido more on point than at the Renwick Smallpox Hospital, a crumbling three-story, U-shaped monster on the southern tip of Roosevelt Island.

Once a marvel of neo-Gothic architecture, Renwick was now a rotting stone carcass, the final way station for thirteen thousand men, women, and children who had died a painful death.

For the city fathers, Renwick was a historical landmark. For the urban explorers, it was New York's most haunted house. But for Aubrey Davenport, it was a sexual Mecca, and on a warm evening in early May, she and a willing partner scaled the eight-foot fence, made their way into the bowels of the moldering labyrinth, and spread a thick quilted blanket on the rocky floor.

She kicked off her shoes, removed her shirt and bra, shucked her jeans, and stood there, naked except for a pair of aquamarine bikini panties.

Her nipples responded to the caress of a cool breeze that drifted over her breasts, and she inhaled the earthy scent of the decay around her, mixed with the dank overtones of river water.

She dropped to her knees on the blanket, closed her eyes, and waited for her partner.

She shuddered as he silently slipped the noose around her neck. His fingers were long and slender. *Piano player fingers,* her mother used to call them. *Like your father has.*

As a child, Aubrey wondered why a man blessed with the hands of a concert pianist never played an instrument, never even cared to. But somewhere along the way she came to understand that Cyril Davenport's long, slender fingers made music of another kind: the crescendo of sound that came from her parents' bedroom on a nightly basis.

Aubrey felt the rope pull tighter. Rope was a misnomer. It was a long strand of silk—the belt from a robe, perhaps—and it felt soft and smooth as he cinched it against her carotid arteries.

He took her shoulders and guided her body to the ground until her belly was flat against the cotton blanket below her.

"Comfy?" he asked.

She laughed. *Comfy* was such a dumb word.

"You're laughing," he said. "Life is good, yes?"

"Mmmmmm," she responded.

"It's about to get better," he said, tugging at the waistband of her panties and sliding them down to her ankles. His fingers teased as they walked slowly up her leg and came to rest on the patch of ink etched into her thigh. His thumb stroked the shrouded figure and arced along the scythe that was clutched in its bony claw.

"Hello, death," he said, removing his hand.

Crack! The cat-o'-nine-tails lashed across her bare bottom, burning, stinging, each individual knotted-leather strap leaving its mark. She bit down hard and buried a scream into the blanket.

Pain was the appetizer. Pleasure was the main course. Her body tensed as she waited for his next move.

In a single, practiced motion he bent her legs at the knees, tipped them back toward her head, grabbed the tether that was around her neck, and tied the other end to her ankles.

"Hand," he ordered.

Aubrey, her right arm beneath her stomach, reached all the way down until her hand was between her legs.

"Life is good," he repeated. "Make it better."

Her fingers groped, parting the pleats, entering the canal, tantalizing the nerve endings. The effect was dizzying: the man with the whip, the foul-smelling ruins, and the inescapable presence of thirteen thousand dead souls.

He said something, but she couldn't hear over the sound of her own labored breathing. And then—the point of no return. She felt the swell of gratification surging through her body, and with near surgical precision she gently lowered her feet toward the ground.

The silk rope around her neck tightened, compressing her carotid arteries. The sudden loss of oxygen along with the buildup of carbon dioxide made her light-headed, giddy, almost hallucinogenic. The orgasm came in waves. It left her gasping for air, but the euphoria was so powerful, so addictive, that she intensified the pressure around her neck, knowing she could go just a few more seconds.

If erotic asphyxiation were an Olympic event, Aubrey Davenport would have been a world-class contender. Her brain was just on the threshold of losing consciousness when she released the death grip, and brought her feet back toward her buttocks.

But the noose refused to relax. If anything, it felt tighter. Panic seized her. She thrashed, pulled her hands up to her throat, and clawed at the silk, fighting for air and finding none.

She never made mistakes. Something must have snagged. She reached behind her neck, desperately trying to find some slack, when her fingers found his hand. He jerked hard on the silk cord, and her arms flailed.

She slumped, too weak to struggle, all hope gone. Everything went black, and as the reaper stepped out of the darkness to claim her, tears streamed down her cheeks, because in the last seconds of her life, Aubrey Davenport finally realized that she didn't want to die.

THE COTILLION ROOM at The Pierre hotel bubbled over with New York's wealthiest—including a few who were wealthier than some countries.

They were the richest of the rich, the ones who get invited to fifty-thousand-dollars-a-plate dinners when one of their own wants to tap them for a worthy cause. In this case, the charity with its hand out was the Silver Bullet Foundation.

The thirty-foot-long banner at the front of the hall proclaimed its noble mission: FIGHTING FOR THE LESS FORTUNATE.

The man in the black tie and white jacket busing tables in the rear had boiled when he first saw the sign. *They haven't done shit for me, and I'm the least fortunate person in the room.*

They're like swans, he thought as he watched them glide serenely from table to table: *so elegant, so regal, but fiercely territorial and vicious when they feel threatened. And like swans,* he observed, *they are oh so white.*

He counted half a dozen black swans among them, but for the most part, the people of color were there to serve. He fit right in.

With his shoulders slumped, his jaw slack, and a cheap pair of clear-lens nerd glasses to dial down the intensity of his piercing black eyes, he was practically invisible, and definitely forgettable.

The only human contact he'd had in the three hours since donning the uniform was with a besotted old patrician who'd slurred, "Hey fella, where's the men's room?"

Shortly after nine, the lights dimmed, the chatter died down, and the commanding voice of James Earl Jones piped through the sound system.

"Ladies and gentlemen, please welcome the cofounder and chairman of the Silver Bullet Foundation, Mr. Princeton Wells."

The staff had been instructed to stop work during the presentation, and the busboy dutifully stepped into the shadows near a fire exit as Princeton Wells bounded onto the stage.

Wells was his typically charming, still-boyish-at-forty, old-moneyed self. And lest any man in the room suspect that someone that rich and that good-looking wasn't getting laid, Wells kicked off the festivities by introducing his current girlfriend, Kenda Whithouse, to a captive audience.

Ms. Whithouse stood up, waved to the room, and threw her billionaire boyfriend a kiss. She was only twenty-three, an actress who was not quite yet tabloid fodder, but who clearly had the talent to fill out an evening gown. Those who knew Princeton Wells had no doubt that the gown would be lying crumpled on his bedroom floor by morning.

Having trotted out his latest eye candy, Wells got down to the serious business of reminding all the do-gooders in the room how much good they were doing for the city's less fortunate.

"And no one," he decreed, "has been more supportive of Silver Bullet than Her Honor, the mayor of New York, Muriel Sykes."

The city's first female mayor, her approval rating still sky-high after only four months in office, was greeted by enthusiastic applause as she stepped up to the podium.

The busboy did not applaud. He slid his smartphone from his jacket pocket and tapped six digits onto the keypad.

One, two, two, nine, nine, seven.

He stared at it, not seeing a sequence of numbers but a moment in time that had changed his life forever: December 29, 1997. His finger hovered over the Send button as the mayor began to speak.

"I'm not a big fan of giving speeches at rubber chicken dinners," she said, "even when the chicken turns out to be grade A5 Miyazaki Wagyu beef."

Everyone but the busboy found that funny.

"On the second day of my administration, I had a meeting with the four founders of Silver Bullet. They showed me a picture of an abandoned old warehouse in the Bronx, and I said, 'Who owns that eyesore?' And they said, 'You do, Madam Mayor. But if you sell it to us for a dollar, we will raise enough money to convert it into permanent housing for a hundred and twenty-five chronically homeless adults.'

"I accepted their offer, framed the dollar, and am thrilled to announce that next month we will start construction. I'm here tonight to thank you all for your generous contributions and to introduce one of the four men who spearheaded this project. He is the brilliant architect whose vision will turn that dilapidated monstrosity into a beautiful apartment complex for some of our neediest citizens. Ladies and gentlemen, please welcome Del Fairfax."

Fairfax, architect to the one percent, stepped onto the stage to show off what wonders he could create for the indigent. Spot-on handsome and aw-shucks personable, he rested a laptop on the podium, flipped it open, and said, "I know how fond you all are of PowerPoint presentations, so I put one together for you. Only ninety-seven slides."

The half-sloshed crowd warmly gave him his due.

"Just kidding," he said. "Princeton told me if I showed more than five, you'd start asking for your money back. The new facility will be called Tremont Gardens. First, let me show you what it looks like now."

He picked up a wireless remote and pushed a button.

The explosion rocked the Cotillion Room.

Del Fairfax's upper torso hurtled toward the screen behind him, while the bomb's jet spray of ball bearings, nails, and glass shards chewed into his lower half, scattering bits and pieces across the stage like a wood chipper gone rogue.

Thick smoke, flying shrapnel, and abject fear filled the air.

The busboy, standing far from the backblast, slipped through the emergency exit, leaving in his wake sheer pandemonium, as four hundred New Yorkers found themselves caught up in the nightmare they had been dreading since September 11, 2001.

The People vs. Alex Cross

James Patterson

The charges: explosive

Alex Cross has never been on the wrong side of the law – until now. Charged with gunning down followers of his nemesis Gary Soneji in cold blood, Cross is being turned into the poster child for trigger-happy cops who think they're above the law.

The evidence: shocking

As Cross fights for his freedom, his former partner John Sampson brings him a gruesome video tied to the mysterious disappearances of several young girls. Despite his suspension from the department, Cross can't say no to Sampson, even if it may end up costing him what's left of his career.

The People vs. Alex Cross: the trial of the century

As the prosecution presents its case, and the nation watches, even those closest to Cross begin to doubt his innocence. Although he has everything on the line, Cross will do whatever it takes to stop a dangerous criminal . . . even if he can't save himself.

CENTURY

THE NEW NOVEL IN THE DETECTIVE
MICHAEL BENNETT SERIES, AVAILABLE NOW IN HARDBACK

Haunted

James Patterson
& James O. Born

**You can take Michael Bennett out of
New York City, but you can't take the cop out
of Michael Bennett.**

Detective Michael Bennett is ready for a
vacation after a series of crises push him,
and his family, to the brink.

He settles on an idyllic small town in the
beautiful Maine woods. But just when Bennett
thinks he can relax, he gets pulled into a case
that has shocked the tight-knit community. Kids
are disappearing with no explanation – until
several bodies turn up in the woods.

Far from the city streets he knows so well,
Bennett is fighting to protect a town, the law,
and the family that he loves above all else.

CENTURY

FOLLOW-UP TO THE *SUNDAY TIMES*
BESTSELLER *NEVER NEVER*

Fifty Fifty

James Patterson
& Candice Fox

**It's not easy being a good detective . . .
when your brother's a serial killer.**

Sam Blue stands accused of the brutal murders of
three young students, their bodies dumped near
the Georges River. Only one person believes he is
innocent: his sister, Detective Harriet Blue. And she's
determined to prove it.

Except she's now been banished to the outback town
of Last Chance Valley (population 75), where a diary
found on the roadside outlines a shocking plan – the
massacre of the entire town. And the first death,
shortly after Harry's arrival, suggests the clock is
already ticking.

Meanwhile, back in Sydney, a young woman holds the
key to crack Sam's case wide open.

**If only she could escape the madman
holding her hostage . . .**

CENTURY

Also by James Patterson

ALEX CROSS NOVELS

Along Came a Spider • Kiss the Girls • Jack and Jill • Cat and Mouse • Pop Goes the Weasel • Roses are Red • Violets are Blue • Four Blind Mice • The Big Bad Wolf • London Bridges • Mary, Mary • Cross • Double Cross • Cross Country • Alex Cross's Trial (*with Richard DiLallo*) • I, Alex Cross • Cross Fire • Kill Alex Cross • Merry Christmas, Alex Cross • Alex Cross, Run • Cross My Heart • Hope to Die • Cross Justice • Cross the Line • The People vs. Alex Cross

DETECTIVE MICHAEL BENNETT SERIES

Step on a Crack (*with Michael Ledwidge*) • Run for Your Life (*with Michael Ledwidge*) • Worst Case (*with Michael Ledwidge*) • Tick Tock (*with Michael Ledwidge*) • I, Michael Bennett (*with Michael Ledwidge*) • Gone (*with Michael Ledwidge*) • Burn (*with Michael Ledwidge*) • Alert (*with Michael Ledwidge*) • Bullseye (*with Michael Ledwidge*) • Haunted (*with James O. Born*)

PRIVATE NOVELS

Private (*with Maxine Paetro*) • Private London (*with Mark Pearson*) • Private Games (*with Mark Sullivan*) • Private: No. 1 Suspect (*with Maxine Paetro*) • Private Berlin (*with Mark Sullivan*) • Private Down Under (*with Michael White*) • Private L.A. (*with Mark Sullivan*) • Private India (*with Ashwin Sanghi*) • Private Vegas (*with Maxine Paetro*) • Private Sydney (*with Kathryn Fox*) • Private Paris (*with Mark Sullivan*) • The Games (*with Mark Sullivan*) • Private Delhi (*with Ashwin Sanghi*)

NYPD RED SERIES

NYPD Red (*with Marshall Karp*) • NYPD Red 2 (*with Marshall Karp*) • NYPD Red 3 (*with Marshall Karp*) • NYPD Red 4 (*with Marshall Karp*) • NYPD Red 5 (*with Marshall Karp*)

DETECTIVE HARRIET BLUE SERIES

Never Never (*with Candice Fox*) • Fifty Fifty (*with Candice Fox*)

STAND-ALONE THRILLERS

The Thomas Berryman Number • Hide and Seek • Black Market •The Midnight Club • Sail (*with Howard Roughan*) • Swimsuit (*with Maxine Paetro*) • Don't Blink (*with Howard Roughan*) • Postcard Killers (*with Liza Marklund*) • Toys (*with Neil McMahon*) • Now You See Her (*with Michael Ledwidge*) • Kill Me If You Can (*with Marshall Karp*) • Guilty Wives (*with David Ellis*) • Zoo (*with Michael Ledwidge*) • Second Honeymoon (*with Howard Roughan*) • Mistress (*with David Ellis*) • Invisible (*with David Ellis*) • Truth or Die (*with Howard Roughan*) • Murder House (*with David Ellis*) • Woman of God (*with Maxine Paetro*) • The Black Book (*with David Ellis*) • Murder Games (*with Howard Roughan*) • The Store (*with Richard DiLallo*) • The Moores are Missing (*with Loren D. Estleman, Sam Hawken and Ed Chatterton*) • The Family Lawyer (*with Robert Rotstein, Christopher Charles and Rachel Howzell Hall*)

ROMANCE

Sundays at Tiffany's (*with Gabrielle Charbonnet*) • The Christmas Wedding (*with Richard DiLallo*) • First Love (*with Emily Raymond*) • Two from the Heart (*with Frank Costantini, Emily Raymond and Brian Sitts*)

NON-FICTION

Torn Apart (*with Hal and Cory Friedman*) • The Murder of King Tut (*with Martin Dugard*) • All-American Murder (*with Alex Abramovich and Mike Harvkey*)

MURDER IS FOREVER TRUE CRIME

Murder, Interrupted (*with Alex Abramovich and Christopher Charles*) • Home Sweet Murder (*with Andrew Bourelle and Scott Slaven*) • Murder Beyond the Grave (*with Andrew Bourelle and Christopher Charles*)

OTHER TITLES

Miracle at Augusta (*with Peter de Jonge*) • Penguins of America (*with Jack Patterson*)

FAMILY OF PAGE-TURNERS

MIDDLE SCHOOL BOOKS

The Worst Years of My Life (*with Chris Tebbetts*) • Get Me Out of Here! (*with Chris Tebbetts*) • My Brother Is a Big, Fat Liar (*with Lisa Papademetriou*) • How I Survived Bullies, Broccoli, and Snake Hill (*with Chris Tebbetts*) • Ultimate Showdown (*with Julia Bergen*) • Save Rafe! (*with Chris Tebbetts*) • Just My Rotten Luck (*with Chris Tebbetts*) • Dog's Best Friend (*with Chris Tebbetts*) • Escape to Australia (*with Martin Chatterton*)

I FUNNY SERIES

I Funny (*with Chris Grabenstein*) • I Even Funnier (*with Chris Grabenstein*) • I Totally Funniest (*with Chris Grabenstein*) • I Funny TV (*with Chris Grabenstein*) • School of Laughs (*with Chris Grabenstein*)

TREASURE HUNTERS SERIES

Treasure Hunters (*with Chris Grabenstein*) • Danger Down the Nile (*with Chris Grabenstein*) • Secret of the Forbidden City (*with Chris Grabenstein*) • Peril at the Top of the World (*with Chris Grabenstein*) • Quest for the City of Gold (*with Chris Grabenstein*)

HOUSE OF ROBOTS SERIES

House of Robots (*with Chris Grabenstein*) • Robots Go Wild! (*with Chris Grabenstein*) • Robot Revolution (*with Chris Grabenstein*)

JACKY HA-HA SERIES

Jacky Ha-Ha (*with Chris Grabenstein*) • My Life is a Joke (*with Chris Grabenstein*)

OTHER ILLUSTRATED NOVELS

Kenny Wright: Superhero (*with Chris Tebbetts*) • Homeroom Diaries (*with Lisa Papademetriou*) • Word of Mouse (*with Chris Grabenstein*) • Pottymouth and Stoopid (*with Chris Grabenstein*) • Laugh Out Loud (*with Chris Grabenstein*)

MAXIMUM RIDE SERIES

The Angel Experiment • School's Out Forever • Saving the World and Other Extreme Sports • The Final Warning • Max • Fang • Angel • Nevermore • Forever

CONFESSIONS SERIES

Confessions of a Murder Suspect (*with Maxine Paetro*) • The Private School Murders (*with Maxine Paetro*) • The Paris Mysteries (*with Maxine Paetro*) • The Murder of an Angel (*with Maxine Paetro*)

WITCH & WIZARD SERIES

Witch & Wizard (*with Gabrielle Charbonnet*) • The Gift (*with Ned Rust*) • The Fire (*with Jill Dembowski*) • The Kiss (*with Jill Dembowski*) • The Lost (*with Emily Raymond*)

DANIEL X SERIES

The Dangerous Days of Daniel X (*with Michael Ledwidge*) • Watch the Skies (*with Ned Rust*) • Demons and Druids (*with Adam Sadler*) • Game Over (*with Ned Rust*) • Armageddon (*with Chris Grabenstein*) • Lights Out (*with Chris Grabenstein*)

OTHER TITLES

Cradle and All • Crazy House (*with Gabrielle Charbonnet*) • Expelled (*with Emily Raymond*)

GRAPHIC NOVELS

Daniel X: Alien Hunter (*with Leopoldo Gout*) • Maximum Ride: Manga Vols. 1–9 (*with NaRae Lee*)

PICTURE BOOKS

Give Please a Chance (*with Bill O'Reilly*) • Big Words for Little Geniuses (*with Susan Patterson*) • Give Thank You a Try • The Candies Save Christmas

For more information about James Patterson's novels, visit
www.jamespatterson.co.uk

Or become a fan on Facebook

MEET THE WOMEN'S MURDER CLUB

Four women sit at their usual table in Susie's bar, and the conversation, as always, is murder…

LINDSAY BOXER

A homicide detective in the San Francisco Police Department, juggling the worst murder cases with the challenges of being a first-time mother. Her loving husband Joe, baby daughter Julie and loyal border-collie Martha give her a reason to protect the city. She's not had the easiest start in life, with an absent father and an ill mother, and she doesn't shy away from a difficult career. Keeping control of her head and her heart can be tough, but with the help of her friends, Lindsay makes it her mission to solve the toughest cases.

CLAIRE WASHBURN

Chief Medical Examiner for San Francisco and one of Lindsay's oldest friends. Wise, confident and viciously funny, she can be relied on to help, whatever the problem. She virtually runs the Office of the Coroner for her overbearing, credit-stealing boss, but rarely complains. You may hear her called 'Butterfly' thanks to a tattoo just below her waist. Happily married with children, her personal life is relatively calm in comparison to her time in the Women's Murder Club.

CINDY THOMAS

An up-and-coming journalist who's always looking for the next big story. She'll go the extra mile, risking life and limb to get her scoop. Sometimes she prefers to grill her friends over cocktails for a juicy secret, but, luckily for them, she's totally trustworthy – most of the time… She's just published a book, somehow finding the time to write between solving cases, writing articles for the *San Francisco Chronicle* and keeping her on–off relationship with Lindsay's partner, Rich Conklin, together. Other than reading, she loves yoga and jazz music.

YUKI CASTELLANO

One of the best lawyers in the city, and desperate to make her mark. Ambitious, intelligent and passionate, she'll fight for what's right, defending the underdog even if it means standing in the way of those she loves. Often this includes her husband – who is also Lindsay's boss – Lt. Jackson Brady. Her friends can barely get a word in edgeways when she's around, unless she's got a Germain-Robin sidecar in her hand!

WHEN YOUR JOB IS MURDER, YOU NEED FRIENDS YOU CAN COUNT ON.